GOD
of the
GRAY AREA

GOD
of the
GRAY AREA

NAVIGATING FAITH AND TRAGEDY

TREVOR M. WILLIAMS

God of the Gray Area
Navigating Faith and Tragedy
© 2024 by Trevor M. Williams

Scriptures marked NKJV are taken from the NEW KING JAMES VERSION (NKJV): Unless otherwise noted, scripture is taken from the NEW KING JAMES VERSION®. Copyright© 1982 by Thomas Nelson, Inc. Used by permission. All rights reserved.

Printed in the United States of America.

Paperback ISBN-13: 979-8-218-46171-3
Hardcover ISBN-13: 979-8-218-48841-3

Library of Congress Control Number: 2024913032

TMW Ministries
York, Pennsylvania

CONTENTS

DEDICATION

As this book has taken me through such an emotional journey, my eyes water up as I write these words. To my beautiful wife LaToia, who has graduated into the LORD's care. You meant so much to me. My life did a complete pivot from the day, I first met you. You inspired me. You loved me with grace and care. You were perfect for me. You love me through my highs and lows, and my great and not so great moments. You were a counterbalanced to my life. You held me accountable to the word of God, making sure that I was standing as the priest of my home you were worth protecting with all of my life.

My heart is broken because I can only share this accomplishment of writing this book with you in spirit. Regardless of how many copies of this book that I sell, how many stages or platforms that I may have the opportunity to speak, any podcasts, radio, or broadcasts I am invited to share my story, it will always feel hollow because I will never be able to share the success with you, or have you embrace me after speaking or preaching. I'll give this ode to you. This is my offering of my heart and life spent with you.

I pray that the words in this book and the things that I may speak well of you would inspire others in a way that would help them to look at life differently and the way they may live life from this point on. Thank you for the life that you share with me.

FOREWORD

I had just walked into the thumping beat of a celebratory worship service when I received a jarring text message. Our good friends, Trevor and LaToia Williams, and their three children had been in a car accident. LaToia did not make it.

The thump of the drums became noise, obnoxious, and strangely, insincere. *How can the God who is the Saints' Protector and Refuge be praised in a time like this?*

Five went out that day for a time of family fun. Fate crashed the party, leaving only four. Trevor, Beautiful, Trenton, and Marquiś must remain, but LaToia was snatched away behind that dark, foreboding veil we humans foolishly call the *after*-life.

LaToia embodied the gentle love and beauty of Jesus. Though by nature an introvert, gentleness, joy, and goodness were in her bones. She was a *beautiful* human being.

When my wife, Gail, and I first met LaToia, we were introduced to her as Mrs. Williams. She was to be the first-grade teacher to our firstborn son at a new school he was attending called Logos Academy.

We decided to send our little Ellis to Logos Academy because of the cultural diversity of the student body. We were full of joy upon finding that his first teacher was a Black woman. We would soon learn that Mrs. Williams was so much more than her Blackness.

LaToia understood her role in God's glorious narrative as an unashamed, passionate worshipper. While most of us choose that one most flattering photo of ourselves in just the right light, with just the right photogenic angle for our Facebook profile image, LaToia picked a black and white image of herself on her knees, back to the camera, with arms stretched wide in a worship service.

Yes, LaToia was a Black woman, a wife, a mom, a daughter, a neighbor, a teacher, a Church member, and a friend, but more than that—surpassing these roles—she was a *vessel*. LaToia was the kind of available, moldable, eager-to-be-used kind of vessel in whom God delights.

We are not privy to how or why God uses certain vessels. Some earthen vessels, like porcelain china and crystal wine goblets, are created for special occasions. They are beautiful, enduring, and to be put on display in a cabinet for visitors to see and enjoy.

Other earthen vessels, like red solo cups, are flimsy, temporary, and disposable, better suited for a backyard barbecue. You will not find a cabinet for displaying red solo cups.

Crystal wine goblets are designed to hold a Napa Valley red, full of depth and flavors to be savored by the palettes of discerning connoisseurs.

A red solo cup is more suited for cheap beer to be guzzled by distracted partygoers.

The discerning connoisseur knew there was something special about this earthen vessel named LaToia Williams. She held within her something unique.

LaToia possessed a surprising *beauty* that was persistently lauded and captured at her celebration of life. The themes and messages from every participant in that service felt strangely coordinated, though they were not. Each of us testified, that, in LaToia, we had beheld something mysterious, a strange and true sort of beauty.

It went beyond the kind of beauty titillatingly splashed on the covers of fashion magazines. LaToia's beauty was not the kind of beauty that could be exploited. Few in this modern age of lust and fleeting pleasure have ever savored this kind of beauty, for if they did but sample a taste, an eternal thirst would be awakened within them for which no earthly drink could satisfy.

How can one say that when you came to a human like LaToia, you were at once encountering a situated-in-time, ordinary, human being, but in actuality, you were beholding a Fountain, an endless Well of Life? The observation almost rises to the charge of blasphemy.

In times like these, of a desperate search for understanding, we need painters and poets to help us utter what ordinary speech fails to capture.

The poet Gerard Manley Hopkins captures these kinds of sentiments in his poem titled *As Kingfishers Catch Fire.*

As kingfishers catch fire, dragonflies draw flame;

As tumbled over rim in roundy wells

Stones ring; like each tucked string tells, each hung bell's

Bow swung finds tongue to fling out broad its name;

Each mortal thing does one thing and the same:

Deals out that being indoors each one dwells;

Selves — goes itself; myself it speaks and spells,

Crying Whát I dó is me: for that I came.

I say móre: the just man justices;

Keeps grace: thát keeps all his goings graces;

Acts in God's eye what in God's eye he is —

Chríst — for Christ plays in ten thousand places,

Lovely in limbs, and lovely in eyes not his

To the Father through the features of men's faces.

This tiny earthen vessel, LaToia, held within her a Beauty that is but whispered by Spring's blooms. In breathy tones, they speak gently of True Beauty, the Rose of Sharon, the Lily of the Valleys, Jesus Christ their Maker.

Christ plays in ten thousand places,

Lovely in limbs, and lovely in eyes not his

To the Father through the features of men's faces.

Christ played a beautiful tune with LaToia's few earthly days. Like Spring's blooms, LaToia's life gently whispered the Beauty of Christ.

The distracted fool of this world, surrounded by constant buzz and noise, would have missed LaToia's whispers. The discerning connoisseur, who has also tasted from the Well, sensed within LaToia an echo, Deep calling to Deep, as Christ played in ten thousand places.

When we vision-impaired, living on this side of the veil, learned of LaToia's death, it felt like priceless porcelain china had been wastefully tossed on a stone floor, scattered pieces never to be restored. As the people of Christ, we must, and boldly do, reject this foolhardy narrative.

No! LaToia's death was not a shattering of pieces never to be restored, but an explosion of glorious beauty that we were privileged to witness. It took LaToia's death for us vision-impaired to begin to understand how it was actually *Jesus* who was *Lovely in LaToia's limbs, and lovely in LaToia's eyes.*

LaToia's life was one of those ten thousand places in which Christ wistfully played. The risen Jesus is not done playing on Earth's terrain.

Jesus is still playfully dancing on earth's spaces some 2,000 years after His death. He tauntingly sings, *"Where O death is your victory? Where O grave is your sting?"*

Death intends to stamp out, silence, and permanently disfigure God's beauty. We initially thought this was what happened to LaToia. Death has no such power.

Christ the Lord had planned something better. LaToia's entrance beyond the veil was a fireworks display of Christ's beauty, each glowing testimony at her celebration of life a dazzling, glimmering show of how He had wistfully played in her quiet life.

LaToia is not in the *after*-life. That phrase is a terrible misnomer. No! LaToia has entered True Life.

There is one passage in CS Lewis's *The Great Divorce* that could have been written of LaToia.

Without ruining the story for you, *The Great Divorce* is about a group of dead people on a bus tour who have the opportunity to visit heaven. After a brief time touring, the narrator witnesses a glorious parade of dazzling creatures and children in honor of a woman who he mistakenly believes to have been a famous human. He is corrected by his guide.

"Is it?...is it?" I whispered to my guide.

"Not at all," said he. "It's someone ye'll never have heard of. Her name on earth was Sarah Smith and she lived at Golders Green."

"She seems to be...well, a person of particular importance?"

"Aye. She is one of the great ones. Ye have heard that fame in this country and fame on Earth are two quite different things."

"And who are these gigantic people...look! They're like emeralds...who are dancing and throwing flowers before here?"

"Haven't ye read your Milton? A thousand liveried angels lackey her." "And who are all these young men and women on each side?"

"They are her sons and daughters."

"She must have had a very large family, Sir."

"Every young man or boy that met her became her son — even if it was only the boy that brought the meat to her back door. Every girl that met her was her daughter."

"Isn't that a bit hard on their own parents?"

"No. There are those that steal other people's children. But her motherhood was of a different kind. Those on whom it fell went back to their natural parents loving them more. Few men looked on her without becoming, in a certain fashion, her lovers. But it was the kind of love that made them not less true, but truer, to their own wives."

"And how...but hullo! What are all these animals? A cat-two cats-dozens of cats. And all those dogs...why, I can't count them. And the birds. And the horses."

"They are her beasts."

"Did she keep a sort of zoo? I mean, this is a bit too much."

"Every beast and bird that came near her had its place in her love. In her they became themselves. And now the abundance of life she has in Christ from the Father flows over into them."

I looked at my Teacher in amazement.

"Yes," he said. "It is like when you throw a stone into a pool, and the concentric waves spread out further and further. Who knows where it will end? Redeemed humanity is still young, it has hardly come to its full strength. But already there is joy enough in the little finger of a great saint such as yonder lady to waken all the dead things of the universe into life."

The ordinary-on-earth Sarah Smith has been transformed into a glorious being. She has *"joy enough in her little finger...to waken all the dead things of the universe into life."*

Sarah's quiet, normal life garnered Heaven's attention. Her simple love and devotion overflowed in life to boys, girls, animals, and to everyone who met her. Sarah is famous in Heaven, one of the great ones.

Sarah Smith and LaToia Williams are one-of-a-kind, simple, earthen vessels, available, and eager to be used by the Christ joyfully looking to play in just one more place.

LaToia is now one of Heaven's great ones.

I used to wonder as a child what we would do in Heaven as if it would be boring and dull. Lewis helped me answer that question. I now know that we will be fully occupied and enraptured as we enjoy Heavenly parades and celebrations of extraordinary people the world has never had the joy of knowing.

People like LaToia Elizabeth Williams.

The book you are holding is the recollection of my good friend Trevor Williams who had the earthly joy of calling LaToia his wife.

This book will tell you the struggle of a man who has held Beauty only to have it snatched away. There is a real, painful, human agony for Trevor in the shift from having known and held Beauty to living out days with constant reminders of her and the empty spaces she used to occupy.

But my brother Trevor has also tasted from the well. Deep calls to Deep. The Christ who played in LaToia is not done playing in Trevor. A Thirst has been awakened within him that no earthly drink can satisfy.

While our earthly funerals are one of God's temporary fireworks shows, can you imagine the glory and splendor that will be made known to us on the Last Day? On that Day, we will be eyewitnesses of stories, ten thousand times ten thousand, where Christ played in millions, and even billions of lovely places.

This, my reading friend, is the Glory behind that veil which LaToia has passed.

I hope as you read this testimony of a struggling man clinging to his hope in Christ that you too will discover the strength to carry you through life's vapors of grief as you wait for that Glorious Day.

Take heart! Christ is risen from the Dead. Deep is calling to Deep.

Rev. Aaron J. Anderson
CEO, Logos Academy
Brother and friend of Trevor Williams
Eyewitness of the Beauty of Christ in my friend,
LaToia Williams

INTRODUCTION

Never in my wildest dreams did I think a casual conversation would lead up to the publishing of such a significant book. If I am honest, I didn't really want to write this book. In fact, I wish I didn't have to write it. It is one of those unexpected Godly moments where you can see Him moving and shifting things intentionally. You see God being God and at the same time you don't feel prepared to receive what he is about to do.

After a Godly connection occurred, I ended up having a conversation with Peter Lopez, the owner of *Publify Press*. I was just there pouring my heart out to this man, who for some unknown reason was inspired by my current process and was being used by the Lord. He was pushing me to share my grief, my pain, and my truth with the world. I was genuinely expressing my feelings of not cashing in on my tragedy and although he understood that, he said to me, "This book will outlast you and even your children. The book will be part of your legacy." It was at that point I knew I had to complete this project because "It's bigger than me."

I knew there are people who are experiencing similar scenarios such as mine but never had the words to explain what they are feeling or words to adequately illustrate what they are going through. If I take it even further, death isn't a topic a lot of people are comfortable speaking about. In addition, the healing process from a loss is so significant, so painful and beautiful, so diverse, and so different for every human being. This grief is not shared enough, and even less so through the grace and love of our Lord.

I decided to share with you my story of love to honor the memory of my wife, LaToia Elizabeth Williams, to shed some light on all the events that occurred prior to her passing and how God took care of every single detail before, during, and to this day as I write these words for you. I have learned in this season, how by revealing your heart and your toughest times, it helps you to overcome unexpected trials and events that come forth.

When life comes at you unexpectedly, you might not feel prepared for the outcome, but it has been through this unexpected process where my faith has strengthened, and I am now seeing purpose. I never truly understood the *'beauty in ashes'* term until this very moment. LaToia was such an extraordinary, virtuous woman that it comes as no surprise to me that even her passing has a deeper purpose. It is the base of what God will use so that you can find inspiration once again, so that you regain hope, push towards the pain, and understand that God sits with us in our mourning process.

The word of God says in Amos 3:7 *"Indeed, the Sovereign Lord never does anything until he reveals his plans to his servants the prophets."* Many times, God speaks to us in preparation for things to come, yet we don't fully understand Him until we are in the midst of the storm, then His words make themselves real in our Spirit and we know He was speaking into our lives. On June 19, 2021, God had set the scenario for me to bring a sermon to the church which I had titled "Heart of the Father," not knowing the verse on which this message was based was the beginning of God's message to my spirit and not the men present in this conference. The Sermon that morning was titled Fight. This was first of two letter that the apostle Paul wrote to his young understudy, Timothy. Though Timothy was young, Paul knew he was equipped enough to handle the challenges that faced the young leader of the new faith community. In 1 Timothy 6:12 it says:

"Fight the good fight of faith. Take hold of a life that lasts forever. You were chosen to receive it. You have spoken well about this life in front of many people."

The Apostle Paul understood the level of attacks Timothy would face moving forward in establishing a healthy faith community would be weighty. In the region in which he served, he would be physically, emotionally, and intellectually challenged. He would have to fight against false teaching and stand firm to protect the spiritual integrity of the flock. If any of you have ever been in a fight, you know that no one comes to a fight with good intentions involved.

I started the sermon with a boxing scene from a fight between Deontay Wilder and Tyson Fury, where late twelfth round, Wilder knocks Fury down. When the referee is on the official countdown to declare a loss...5...6...at count number 7, he starts getting up...8...and on count 9, Fury gets up on his feet. The crowd was going wild. People were in disbelief as to how after receiving such a hard blow, with the capacity of laying him flat on his back, he found the strength to get back up. Everyone watching thought the fight was over, including the person responsible for the knock-down; but Fury rose again.

I started to speak on how some people have been hit with very strong trials and situations and they have not been able to get back up. These are the blows that other people look at and wonder, how we have survived them. It was so specific to what was to come that when I started speaking on the diverse situations that "could have taken us out," I started mentioning how drugs, **car accidents**, bad relationships, crimes committed, and so many other scenarios have hit us and knocked us out and yet, we were still here. The sermon was based on having to fight the good fight of faith while you are in the middle of the match. I will go deeper into this at a later moment in the book, but this fifty-three-minute sermon was the Lord's way of preparing my spirit for life's strongest blow, and I was less than seven hours away from receiving it. Little did I know that after this powerful message I delivered, my wife would lose her life in a tragic car accident.

We woke up that morning as a family of five, but only four came back home. I want to share with you our grieving process, the Lord's divine intervention, His fidelity, and the purpose and beauty we have discovered amongst the ashes. I am still pushing forward through the process, as it is still an ongoing healing season. Pastor, author, and theologian, Dr. Tony Evans shared the following thought in *Grieving Well:*

> *While we are called to be bold in faith, we must also balance that with the knowledge that we serve a sovereign God, Whose will sometimes require that people we love pass on. We cannot control God. Faith means we must trust even in the face of pain and loss. We must participate with the process of grieving so that those that remain in our lives while on this earth will still have access to our hearts and health, love, and gifts. We must grieve well not only for ourselves and our own healing but for the rest of our loved ones who need us and want us to be present with them.*

And that is exactly what I chose to do. I decided to participate in the healing process for me, my children, my family, friends, faith brothers and sisters and without knowing it at the time, for you. I pray that while you read these pages your spirit can capture the healing power that the Lord has reserved and separated for you. You don't have to lose a person to experience a loss or go through a mourning process to connect with the same pain. Maybe you lost your marriage, your career, your finances, a physical loss, or you lost yourself through personal trauma and you have no idea how to begin picking up the pieces and getting back on your feet. Maybe you have resigned from loving again or believing, you have walked away from your dreams thinking that the adversity. The blow you received was enough to knock you out and keep you on the ground. I am here to testify that overcoming is possible.

After a traumatic event, it is hard for to process what's in front of us. There are some who are trapped in the moment the event happened. This is an example of Post-Traumatic Stress Disorder, or PTSD.. It might just be that the Lord has used my wife's passing and my desire to share our story with the purpose of blessing you. It's never about me, it has always been about Jesus and now, it's about to be a blessing over you. This is our story of overcoming a knockdown on the twelfth round and listening to a countdown that appeared to be declaring a defeat.

"For I am about to do something new. See, I have already begun! Do you not see it? I will make a pathway through the wilderness. I will create rivers in the dry wasteland." - Isaiah 43:19

God will do it again. Just breathe and trust the process. He will never forsake you.

My goal for you is to understand and accept that life is not perfect and it never will be. It's not if turbulence comes—it's *when* it comes. Life will hit you with the punches that you didn't see coming and will make you question everything you've known. It will challenge you in ways you never thought possible. Life will ask the question on the Gatorade commercial: *Is it in you?* My hope is for you to see the ups and downs, the disappointments, struggles, the not-so-perfect moments throughout this process of trauma, grief, and loss through a different perspective.

The biggest takeaway I hope you embrace is knowing that I am not the hero of the story. Grief is a community service project. God places people in your life that will help you walk through difficult moments. There were so many people who played critical roles from the time of the crash to this day and without them the healing process would have been a lot harder. My desire is for everyone to see—despite the good, bad, ugly, and uncomfortable—the GOD who uses all of the ingredients to make and shape us for His purpose. How joy and grief can share the dance floor. I didn't navigate this perfectly, and don't expect you to do it either.

My hope and prayer for you regardless of the grief you endure, is to know that GOD is sitting with you in it. His shoulders are big enough to bear your deepest sorrows, worst frustrations, and that, even when it seems like He isn't listening, He is there and He cares.

"Those who sow in tears shall reap in joy."

Psalms 126:5 NKJV

CHAPTER 1

UNEXPECTED TURNOUTS

On the Saturday morning of June 19, 2021, I woke up super early to pray, add, or subtract anything from the sermon I was preparing for the day. This is the danger of preaching from an iPad–I can add and subtracting things at will as it comes to my mind before coming to the platform. I was scheduled to preach at the Men's Breakfast for Father's Day weekend at our church. I would be preaching about the many fights that life presents you, using a particular fight between Deontae Wilder and Tyson Fury, in which Wilder hits Fury with two-punch combination that had everyone on the ring convinced the fight was over. Fury laid motionless on the ground for 6 ½ seconds, but on the seventh second, he got up, and continued to fight as if you he had never been knocked out. The fight ended in a draw. Many men were impacted by the message. What I didn't realize was how much I would need this sermon in the days ahead.

I came home from the men's breakfast, changed my clothes, and prepared to leave with my family to enjoy Juneteenth festivals in York and Lancaster as well as Father's Day weekend, which was one of my favorite moments to spend time with my family. The "Honey Do" list turned off for the weekend. My wife would always have some kind of gift that I may have said I wanted to get but never came around to get myself. She always added value to my life. I cherished being honored as a father because she valued me as a husband first.

We arrived at the local festival and saw a lot of people we knew. We grabbed some food from local vendors while the kids ran around and played. We left and headed to Lancaster to attend the Black Business Expo. Again, we saw many familiar faces and supported local entrepreneurs. Afterward, we stopped at a few stores in the outlet mall. On our way back, we stopped briefly to see my parents before we headed home for the evening. We gave my dad his Father's Day gift before we headed home. They never imagined this would be the last time my wife would visit my parents, or that they would be the last people to see her.

Trips between York and Lancaster for me were very common; it's like walking around the corner. But this trip, however, was not only uncommon, but life-altering.

As we were driving home, I suddenly noticed a vehicle come off the road into the grass median that separated the eastbound and westbound lanes. I alerted my wife to the vehicle. Our assumption was that the driver would stop because in most cases, I would see a car periodically abandoned in the middle of the median. But this time, the car kept moving and it jumped on our side of the road, into our lane, heading directly for us. We weren't driving fast because we took our smaller vehicle, and it needed a tire rotation. It wobbled when I would try to go 60 mph or above. I could see the car coming but there was nowhere I could turn off because we were just heading into the underpass. The car coming in the opposite direction came so fast, I had no chance to respond. All I remember was a white flash.

I woke up to the sound of sirens around me. I raised my left hand and saw I had blood and major gashes that cut to the bone. I could barely move my body. I was in great pain, but my adrenaline was running so high, I didn't know how bad the situation really was. I looked over to my wife to see if she was okay. The car was folded to where her knees were under her head, she was unconscious, and I saw blood dripping from her head. I tried to reach for her but felt tremendous pain in my right arm. I discovered that my right forearm was shattered. I tried to reach with my other arm, but I couldn't reach her because the pain was so great. I thought my legs were broken by the way the car was crushed on us. I tried to yell for her, but the words couldn't come out of my mouth. I was sitting less than a foot a from the love of my life, but it felt like an eternity away.

Everything started getting loud and confusing. The paramedics had arrived. They asked me for my name. I told them my name. They asked: *"Do you want me to get the kids out?"* I told them to get them out. I immediately asked them to help my wife and they told me, "*I need you to focus on your children right now.*" In my head, I was saying to myself "*What are you talking about?*" I asked them again, "*Forget me, help my wife!*" He repeated to me again, "*Sir, we have to work on getting you and your kids out of the car.*"

And at that moment, I experienced a feeling that I had never felt before in my life. There was one part of me that was still screaming in my head, "*You need to go help my wife.*" The other part of me was realizing what he was trying to do. He was trying to distract me without telling me that my wife was gone. The more it started to settle in that Toia didn't make it, I started to lose consciousness in a way where I was losing my grip on life itself. I felt like my life was fading away from me. In medical terms, I was probably slipping into shock. My thoughts were at war with each other between, "*You 'gotta help her*" and "*My love can't be gone.*"

It was in that moment that I had succumbed to the reality that she was gone, and I was slowly fading out. One moment we were talking about getting the kids ready for bed early that evening when we got home, and in a blink of an eye I was literally fighting for my life. As they were trying to get me out of what was left of our car, I was discovering more injuries. When they put me in the ambulance, all I could think about was the person saying, "*Worry about your children.*" I began to say the name of Jesus over and over and over again. In my complete helplessness, I had nothing left—not a scripture, a sermon, a quote from a book—but the name of Jesus poured out of my mouth. I repeated it until I passed out in the ambulance.

It was a bumpy ride to the hospital, and I was going in and out of consciousness. I remember arriving and seeing my father at Lancaster General. My son was being carted off and sent to Hershey Children's Hospital. I woke up to find myself in a hospital room. I looked up and saw my pastor, Danny Haas, and our operations pastor, Rene Carabello. I looked at the clock and it was 3:44 am. They asked me how I was doing, and I said, *"I feel like I got hit by a car."* At this point, I was still foggy. I knew the kids were still alive but was unsure of their condition besides my middle son, Trenton. My oldest child, Beautiful, and youngest, Marquis', were medivaced to Hershey Childeren's Hospital with life threatening injuries which needed operations.

Pastor Danny delivered the news to me that I never thought I would ever hear: *Toia did not make it.* At that moment, it was like everything stood still. All I could do was sit there. I had tubes connected to me from all over my body, and I was medicated to the high heavens. Was I hearing this correctly? My wife was gone? The woman I spent the last twenty-one years with, building our lives together? Is this even happening? How can this be?

CHAPTER 2

ROAD TOWARDS RECOVERY
& THE WAR WITHIN

The next few days were like a blur between having doctors, other medical practitioners, hospital chaplains, police, family, and friends come in and out of my room. The hospital actually had a strict vistor protocol, but the CEO of the hospital made an exception for me to have as many visitors as I desired.

I believe it was on the third day that I was in the hospital that all the pastoral team came to my room. We sat and talked about a lot of different things. But then I started talking about Toia and how there were so many things that we were looking to do together. For whatever reason, I was just thankful for the twenty-one years of my life I had with her. As I continued to talk about different things, I stepped on the landmine. We were looking forward to paying off the mortgage and having a mortgage burning party. As I began to speak about it, tears welled up in my eyes. My voice broke and I started to weep uncontrollably. All of the plans we were preparing for and thinking we had time to do were all gone. Everything we planned together—gone! Watching our children graduate from high school, college, or the military—gone! Spoiling our grandchildren—gone! It's the nightmare from which I couldn't wake up. It was like those holiday movies you see on the *Hallmark* or *Lifetime* channel, where the main character has some off-beat experience and is transported into a new life without their permission. Except, for me, there was no guardian angel guiding me back to the right path. I couldn't go back. She was gone and I could do anything about it. I felt so helpless. The heaviness of guilt began to settle over me. Why would GOD spare my life and take hers?

As priest and protector of my home, I felt that I should have given up my life for her. Even today, I would still make the trade. I believed I was a failed husband because I couldn't protect my wife. And all I had was a broken-up body to show for it. Twenty-one years of my life with her seemed like a faded memory. I even began to question if I had truly had a wife and lived the life I had. How could this be happening to me?

Whereas you do not know what will happen tomorrow. For what is your life? It is even a vapor that appears for a little time and then vanishes away. (James 4:14)

Though I allowed myself to think that way for the moment, my life did not go up in smoke. But the scripture reminds us that our lives are not as long as they appear to be in grand scheme of things. And when people leave us, it immediately feels as though that there was not enough time. We ask for one more day with them. I thought I had so much time left with her. It felt like wire being ripped out of my system with no repair in sight. It felt like a part of me died that day.

For the next few days, it seemed like a movie that didn't have any *cut to scene* moments. Between nurses coming in and checking my vitals every four to five hours, to family members and friends coming in to visit me—I lost track of what day was very often. Even with COVID protocols in place, the medical staff allowed me to have as many people as I wanted in my room. Thankfully, everyone who visited were people I actually wanted to see. They were people who had invested in me over the years both emotionally and spiritually. Even with all of the support from family and friends, my anxiety was through the roof because my children did not know that their mother had died. They were recovering from surgery, and I only allowed a select few people from the family to be around them. I did not want them to break the news until they were well enough to see me, and I could tell them. I felt as their father, it was my responsibility to be present with them when they heard the worst news of their lives.

Trenton, the middle child and oldest son, who was 10 at the time, was the first to be released. My parents picked him up and headed straight to the hospital where I was staying. When he arrived, I was so happy to see my boy and at the same time felt the crushing weight of having to tell him what happened to his mother. He immediately asked, *"Hey Dad, where's mom?"* As tears started streaming down my face, I began to recap what happened to us. I began to explain about Mommy and how she was hurt very badly in the crash, and how she was not able to recover from her injuries. It was that moment when it clicked for him and he said, *"Mommy died?"* and I nodded my head. He buried his head into my chest, and we began to weep together. I felt so much sorrow for him that he had to find out that his mom was gone. My heart was broken, not only carrying my own sorrow, but the sorrow of our three children who will have to spend the rest of their lives without the woman who nurtured them. After a few minutes, Trenny Boy—which is what we call him at home—raised his head and asked me, *"Dad, does this mean that we are not going to Hershey Park?"* I looked at him like "Are you serious?" I was shocked that he would even ask that question because—to me—it should be the last thing on his mind. But that is how he started coping with the loss. I responded to him saying, *"Dude, we are going to Hershey Park!"* That question broke the tension that hung heavy in the room. The simplicity of a child's life reminded me of when Jesus spoke of having the faith of a little child. Though his heart was broken, the fact that he was in the presence of his father assured him that we would be okay. This was a pivotal moment because it gave me the assurance and the grace to speak to my other children when their time came. The lessons our children teach us are truly priceless.

My youngest child, Marquis, was released a few days after I was transferred to Lancaster Rehabilitation Hospital. I gave him the news of Mommy's passing away, but he wasn't sure what to make of it. I think he was very confused and trying to make sense of what life was going to look like. I wasn't sure what to make of it. He was the baby and he's was a momma's boy; so, I was very concerned giving him the news. It just seemed like he was happy to play with his brother. Thankfully, my dad was off for the summer and my mom being retired allowed them the time to care for then while I was in recovery. They could only do but so much, but my parents would take them all over the place and do different things with them.

Talking to my dad, he said to me, "We have to allow them to be kids. I didn't want them to cooped up in the house all day just for them to sit there and dwell on things." They need to have space to be themselves and not be crowded by people who would grieve all over them. My father was not a stranger to tragedy. He lost two of his older siblings to murder and he saw the affects it had on him and the rest of the family. He understood the emotional toll that it takes.

My oldest and only daughter, Beautiful, had the most physical complications, ended up being in the hospitals for the longest. Her situation, as bleak as it was, revealed how God was still working in the midst of a messy situation. During the accident, she experienced major head trauma to the point that she does not remember the accident to this day. She also had an abdominal tear which ruptured her intestines due to the seatbelts. They cut through her intestinal wall during the crash. She only remembers waking up in the hospital days later. She had a major gash along her right eye, which would leave a nasty scar, but it *just so happened*

God was still working in the midst of a messy situation.

that a plastic surgeon was at Hershey Children's Hospital at the same time that she was being flown in by helicopter. Hershey Children's Hospital *never* has plastic surgeons, so when she arrived, they went to work on her right away. The surgeries were a success and she was expected to make a full recovery. The repair to her eye was such that if you didn't know there was a scar you could barely see it.

All I knew was that I was headed towards a long and slow journey towards recovery, and it wouldn't be just a physical recovery, but was going to include my body, mind, and soul. I had to reprogram and adjust to all aspects of my new reality. I needed to start with the immediate physical therapies, but my mind and soul needed to be cared for as well.

On June 24, 2021, five days after the crash, I was discharged to Lancaster Rehab Hospital for further treatment. I was nowhere close to being able to return home. I was wheeled and loaded into a transport truck. It was a quiet ride. I was lost in my thoughts just trying to make it through the day. I arrived at the rehab center, and it was much quieter than Lancaster General. I didn't know if that was a good thing or a bad thing. From what I could tell, there were not many people my age group in rehab. There wasn't a patient younger than 55 while I was there and yet, there I was, in the same place trying to learn how to walk. It was a very lonely place. Even though I was given relaxed access to have more visitors than the norm, when they left, I was captive to my thoughts.

I had a laundry list of injuries from head to toe:

- I suffered a major head trauma, which caused a jaw misalignment. I was diagnosed with major concussion; however, when I was tested for cognitive abilities, I was scoring well above what was expected.

- My right shoulder and collarbone were misaligned

- A fractured right elbow

- My forearm was broken and splintered in four places. They had to do back-to-back surgeries to keep it from being infected and having it amputated

- The right femur was pushed out of my hip socket and fractured my pelvis

- Strained my IT band (iliotibial band or ITBS) which caused my left leg to swell.

- Torn muscles in in my left ankle.

- Host of scars and bruises on my body.

The nine days of intense therapy were such a humbling experience. The moments I had alone were filled with grief, sadness, doubt, fear, anxiety, and abandonment. Thankfully, Patrina (Simmons) Lewis, a childhood friend, worked in the rehab hospital. She would come and visit me before her shift started. Her visits, conversations, and prayers meant so much to me. There's was such beauty in the LORD sending someone to be with me while I was in such a lonely place. It speaks to GOD's provision in our lives. Every morning, I would be rolled down to the fitness center for my physical therapy sessions. I had to learn how to sit and stand, put one foot in front of the other, go up and down stairs, as if I was a toddler trying to gain balance. I had some complications with my legs because they were swollen from torn muscle tissue.

During one of our morning treatment sessions, I remember working out with a gentleman who had just lost his leg. He said that morning he got out of bed and forgot that he didn't have half of his leg anymore. It was surreal that he was sharing his experience with me. For individuals who have lost limbs, there's a condition called Phantom Limb Syndrome, which happens to 80-100% of amputees, in which they feel the pain or sensation of the limb that does not exist. Often, I hear people who lost their spouse have a similar experience and it can happen at any time. I remember one evening, I went to pick up my phone and automatically called Toia's number, anticipating hearing her voice. It wasn't until about the second ring that I realized what I was doing. I begin to weep uncontrollably. What the man had experienced days earlier when he forgot that he didn't have a portion of his leg, I experienced when I recognized that my wife was gone.

I've been an athlete or a part of something athletically-based for most of my life. During my eight-year career in the US Army, I never scored less than max on my physical training evaluations. Prior to the crash, I ran three to four times a week and went to the gym four days a week while preparing to compete in the US Master's Track & Field Division (aka: the *"ole head track league."*). I've never been in a hospital overnight except for when my wife was in labor with our children. The crash was a shock to my soul in every way. When it came time to continue with my physical therapy, I looked for somebody that I knew would get my body into a functional condition. I asked around and they suggested Pivot Fitness. After the first session, I knew in my heart these were the people who would help me through the journey towards restoration. I documented the process because it was impressive to see that there were so many things I still could not do. Again, it was very humbling seeing how hard it was to get my body back into a physical condition. It is amazing how so many things in our bodies are connected. If one of them is affected or out of line, it causes strain and even injuries in other areas. All I kept asking myself was: "How can I get my body back to be functional?"

All the while, I was also learning a spiritual lesson. I was dwelling on 1 Corinthians 12, which talks about the body of Christ and how every part has its purpose. The Scriptures compares us to the physical body parts and how it is better when everything functions together. In my recovery process, it was not until the actual body parts started to function as they were supposed to that I started seeing progress. Our bodies teach us a lesson about life in that if certain things are out of line, then everything else will be misaligned. When I compared this to my spiritual life how in certain parts of my life can be out of line, everything else is out of line. So, when there is an 'injury' it will cause symptoms that announce that something is wrong. Now it's about looking at the symptoms but rather the root cause of the injury. The real problem is under those symptoms. There are many things in our life that we see as challenges and are basically symptoms of something greater going on within us.

I realized during this process that God is strong enough to handle our weakness. While I was at the gym working on areas of my body I had never concentrated on, the Holy Spirit was doing the same in areas of my mind and soul having my faith exercised. I started to pinpoint areas that were weak, and I had not surrendered. I started to identify areas that I needed to develop further spiritually, or needed rehab because they were tied to trauma in the past. Things and areas that we had never considered to work through natural therapy. The truth is that there are many things we need to work on through Jesus and people. Professionals have studied the human mind through trauma, and God can use through their gifts to help us heal. Our mind and our emotions are also part of our bodies.

I remember being in physical therapy, and the therapist would say: "We work until it hurts." They were not trying to cause another injury but rather teach me the difference between pain and injury. Pain is something we can experience under uncomfortable situations; injury is when we were totally rendered from doing what we normally do. Sometimes we mix up the two and think that we can get passed the pain or push through it. In reality, God will take us sometimes through the pain to heal an injury. There are painful seasons, but through the pain you heal.

July 2, 2021, I was released from the rehab hospital. My mother picked me up and I headed home briefly to swiftly grab some clothes and head to Hershey Medical Center to see about Beauti. I didn't want to linger in my house long because I didn't want to be sucked into the vacuum of emotions I would feel. It was the first time entering my home was a widower.

The day before, I called and talked to my daughter and from what I gathered from the medical team as soon as I spoke to her, the complications that she had begun to subside. It was like she was waiting to hear from me. This was a real spiritual lesson, and that her healing came from hearing the voice of her father. What does that say about us? Hearing from the Father can bring healing to any situation. I arrived Friday evening, and she had a big smile on her face when I arrived.

This was my third and final conversation explaining what happen to their mom. When I broke the news, it was if she already knew but it settled in on her once it was confirmed. We shed our tears all over again, but I felt this sense of relief that all them know about their mother's passing. It wasn't long after our conversation that she rapidly improved in the heath. She was hitting all her benchmarks and evaluations. I came there Friday with the mindset, "I'm to get my daughter out of there." And we left the hospital on Sunday morning. We were finally out of the hospital getting ready to prepare for a new unknown. The day was the 4th of July, 2021.

I was not prepared to go home right away. My children, as they were being released from the hospital, went to my parents' house while I was still in recovery. When we arrived at my parents' house, all three of my children sitting on the couch at the same time. I walked away to my parent's guest room and burst into tears because I recognized that they were all I had. The last time I was here, five of us left and only four came back. I thought I would stay maybe two days with them and then return home. Two days turned into eight days. I just didn't have the strength to go back home. In the long run, it turned out to be the best decision. I feel like if I would've gone home sooner then, we would have gotten bombarded by people and what I really needed was time to regroup.

This was my new reality, my new normal. A father and a man of God whose life partner had gone ahead home to our Heavenly Father. It is hard to re-live the whole incident and the emotions that come with it. Like I mentioned previously, I wish I didn't have the need to share this type of story, this type of testimony with you. I wish I had a simple book of victories and celebrations, like the ones we love to live and share. Yet, this is still is a book of victories, my family's victory through pain and trauma. We discovered the beauty within the ashes. And it is also a celebration. A celebration of the life of LaToia, who even with her passing is still inspiring people with her legacy, her wisdom and through her generations. We have all learned to dance and celebrate under the rain.

"The Lord is near to those who have a broken heart And saves such as have a contrite spirit."

Psalms 34:18 NKJV

CHAPTER 3

LATOIA

"Her husband is known in the gates, when
he sits among the elders of the land."

Proverbs 31:23 NKJV

Twenty-one years together, seventeen married. Looking back, it doesn't seem that long. I still remember the first time I saw her. I was hanging out with my cousin Archie who worked at Millersville University at a summer program. We were hanging out in the lobby of the Student Memorial Center. And then there was this young lady walking by in a blue and white dress and holding a handful of books. When she saw us, she paused and came to say hello to my cousin.

From the first time I saw her, I knew there was something about her that I couldn't shake. I knew there was something special about her. I just did not know how to shake it. I was still figuring out life at that point and, more importantly, I wasn't walking with Christ. The crazy part was when I was going to approach her,

I heard a voice inside of me say *"You can't give her what she needs."* I literally stopped in my tracks and did not pursue her. It was the best thing for both of us. I wasn't in a position to be in a relationship, nor try to complicate her life with my foolishness.

A few months later, after I came back from a homecoming weekend at Morgan State University where my cousin went to school, I started unpacking my clothes. I started feeling just as empty as the bag I had just emptied out of the clothes that I had brought back. The empty bag represented my emptiness spiritually. The smell of weed, alcohol, and sweat came out of the bag. It represented what I was pouring my life into—partying away with no plan for the future. At that moment, I recognized that I was in need of Jesus to fill the major void that I had avoided for so long. On October 17, 1999, I gave my life to Christ by my bedside and I've never looked back.

Not even two months later, I played the drums at a choir concert in Millersville University's Gospel Choir, and I saw her. I instantly knew who she was. I knew this time I was not going to fold like before and hopefully the voice didn't come back which, by this time, I knew was the Holy Spirit. I presented myself and told her that I had met her a few months ago. Even though she didn't remember me, we exchanged numbers.

From the first night we talked on the phone we just fell together perfectly like two puzzle pieces. It was just very easy. I discovered that she was in her junior year and was getting ready to start student teaching.

As for me, I was working at a printing factory and it was not really the thing that I wanted to do. I thought I would've been in college on an athletic scholarship, but life didn't work out like I thought. I saw her pursuing her goals and it made me immediately step my game up. It was only a few weeks after I met her that I went to a recruiting station and enlisted in the United States Army. I needed something to jumpstart my life, but also to keep up with her. If I was going to pursue this relationship, I wanted to have some collateral to present for the future. She was that type of woman! There was no in between. Either you're with her or you're not. I wasn't about to miss out on a good thing (Proverbs 18:22)

"He who finds a wife finds a good thing, and obtains favor from the LORD."

In other words, I saw that she is an asset in my life, from the very beginning, she encouraged and push me to pursue greater things. It caused me to become a leader. As I lead her and potentially lead my household, I must understand the favor and the blessing of the LORD is the things that carries us through.

I knew from the first day that I saw her, she would be my wife. We lived in different cities but it help with our communication because talked to each other everyday. She was sweet, kindhearted, giving, fair, and set such an example of godly womanhood. There was no one like her, and somehow, despite my crazy self, God decided to show this level of grace to my life. She matched my temperament perfectly. She was very low-key and a bit of an introvert, and I was the social butterfly and the High Wire act. She was very supportive. She challenged me when I needed to be challenged. She was my cheerleader in everything that I did. She was an embodiment of Proverbs 31:10-31 in every possible way. "Who can find a virtuous wife? For her worth is far above rubies" (V. 10).

Within two years I was ready to propose for her hand in marriage. On, September 21, 2001, I didn't have enough money at the time to buy a ring. At the time, I living with my parents, a young college student, Army Reservist, and working at the Christian youth center, I was hustling and trying to figuring things out. How am I gonna let her know that I am committed to spending the rest of my life with her? That day, while at my parents house, we were watching TV downstairs in the basement. I went upstairs to make popcorn and I heard the LORD say "Propose, dummy!!" I'm like "How am I propose with I didn't have a ring?

He said' "Use the bowl you were gonna use for popcorn and fill it with water." Immediately, I understood what He wanted. He using this as a symbolic sign of leadership. I came downstairs with a bowl of water, not trying to spill it. She sees me coming down with no popcorn, and she says "What are you up to?" I ask her to take her shoes. I put the towel down and took her feet and began to wash her feet as a sign of servitude. She began to cry and she said yes. .

What I appreciated about her the most was that she was very consistent in many things. Consistency creates reliability, and reliability, trust. I trusted her with everything. I trusted her with my heart and my deepest thoughts that she would never violate that space. I revealed some of the deepest secrets that I had in my life, and she never told anybody, and she never judged me for it. When you love somebody, it's an everyday decision, not a feeling. Marriage counseling helped avoid many pitfalls many married couples are ensnared by. My former pastor, Elder Gerald T. Simmons, M.Div, was our marriage counselor. He was very thorough with his approach to marriage and what it took to sustain a healthy relationship. I still have the packet we worked through to this day. He's said that *"A good counselor's job is to break you up and pull you together."* In other words, pick apart the potential weaknesses and pull together the solution that both can agree upon to use to resolve conflict. This was a game changer.

We were fortunate to have healthy married couples who had been married for quite a while. We were able to gleam from their wisdom and ask questions about scenarios that they encountered on their journey. One of the greatest pieces of advice we received was *"Keep the small things small."* Neither one of us were fans of arguing, though disagreements always happened. It was nowhere near the level of knock'em out, drag'em out altercations I've witnessed. I didn't want that for our marriage.

When we made it public, we vowed to make a covenant and build our lives together. So, on July 17, 2004, we made a decision to love each other every day, even in difficult times. For richer or poor, sickness and health.

Oftentimes we hear these vows at a wedding, and though it sounds deep at the moment, we don't really understand the depth of those phrases. They are feasible in the times when it seems that financially everything's going well and the times where you are looking for spare change in the couch. The times where it seems like you get to go on vacation every summer, and the times when your health does not allow you to go anywhere. Many couples face these realities, and oftentimes, one or both of them check out and do not live up to the vows that they made on their wedding day.

She was a living, breathing example of what scripture means when talking about a wife being a help mate (Genesis 2:18-25). I wouldn't be the person that I am today without the LORD placing her in my life. I wouldn't be the person I am in ministry without her. She allowed me to continue to pursue my degree even though it would take a lot of time from the family, but she knew how important it was for me to finish, and the opportunities that it would create for our household. She was an avid learner, and if she didn't know something, she would educate herself to become more informed about it.

I remember a time about five to six years prior to Toia's passing, I had this overwhelming feeling of anxiety wash over me. It started with the thought, *"If Toia dies, what would I do?"* I didn't know where any important documents were placed in the house. I immediately went to my wife and asked her where she placed them. She went to a dresser that we shared and opened up a drawer that had all of our important documents, including our will and power of attorney, as well as our life insurance policies.

Now, this is going to be a teaching moment. If you are reading this and do not have a life insurance policy or a will, before you finish this book, you need to get one. To be blunt, you are setting up your loved ones for complete failure without them. There's a quote from Pastor Keion Henderson, the lead pastor of the Lighthouse Church in Houston, Texas that rings in my ears. During a sermon, he said, *"We're sick of having to fry chicken to bury you."*

In many ways, he was right! An AARP poll shows that 60 percent of Americans do not have a will/power of attorney and/or life insurance policy (https://www.aarp.org/money/investing/info-2017/half-of-adults-do-not-have-wills.html) There are so many people who are unprepared to die. I know it sounds backwards, but it's not only the expenses that matter, it's everything else that comes after someone passes away. It will be a difficult and an emotional time for the family members, so when you add this to the mix, it can be overwhelming.

Having to prepare for Toia's celebration process was one of the most difficult pieces in the puzzle for me, because I was faced with the reality that she was gone. There I was, sitting with the mortician and as he was handing me some of her belongings that they were able to recover from the crash, it hit home in a way that I could have never imagined. Mind you, I was still broken by the idea of knowing that it only been three weeks since the accident and all these things would never be put to use again. Some of those items still had blood stains on them. It was just a hard pill to swallow, knowing that my wife had to suffer such a horrible death. Although I know that God's grace did not allow her to suffer, it still breaks my heart to this day.

During the process, I had to make a lot of snap decisions that I wish I didn't have to make. This was the time to think of details like where she would be buried. As I was having that conversation with the groundskeeper, I was just full of frustration. All of the technicality of having to make these decisions, having to put out so much money for something so tragic gave me a headache. LaToia and I used to be so intentional with our money by saving up for things we wanted to do, and this was definitely not something we had planned on investing and saving up for. In fact, I was so mad as I looked at the costs of the burial plot, the casket, and a number of other things because we had saved up some money to do other things and now, I was having to bury my wife! A lot of things came to mind at that moment, but I was full of frustration and anger. These feelings lasted the entire day. I now can say that the anger represented the realness of what had happened. I did not fathom this ever being part of my life and it was the moment that it became real and surreal for me. I knew I had to fight through it because my children were expecting me not to quit.

The days leading up to her celebration were filled with other preparations, people calling me, my siblings letting me know they would be coming to be present with us and me letting everyone know where the church was located and a number of other things. It became a burden. The everyday life scenarios were painful. I returned home a week before Toia's celebration and not seeing her present, yet everything in our home spoke about her. It was just a surreal moment that caught me off guard. It's still hard to face at times.

I went to the church and made a thank you video for everyone that contributed in some way or another to our cause and made life during those days just a little bit easier. People were still getting everything prepped and I walked into the gymnasium/fellowship hall, and I saw that they decorated the entire area where they would have the repass. I did not know that they were going to do this. Toia's sister had taken this initiative, who was the main person during all of this celebration. My first thought was, *who is having a wedding?* Everything looked so beautiful and special. They did such a great job putting everything together and there were so many details. It was a lot to take in, yet I saw God in every single detail. It was mind-blowing.

I continued to the sanctuary where the worship team was, along with some people that I had contacted. I had requested specific worship songs and they did not hesitate. I walked in and sat in the back, and just listened to them. They were singing a song from a group called *People and Songs* and the song was basically singing Psalms 23. It had always been one of my favorite songs, but at this moment it became a song I *needed* to hear. They were singing the verse that stated that *"the Lord would restore my soul,"* and those words penetrated my soul. Not only because of the words that were being sung; but rather that the worship team was carrying the weight of our loss. There was a level of *carrying each other's burdens,* and I could feel them carrying the weight with us. So, I just sat there and wept, feeling them carrying us, lifting us up. I decided to go up on the platform and encourage them in such a way and say thank you for what they were contributing. After this moment, all of the frustration and anger I had been carrying around was lifted. I felt God was getting ready to do something that was far beyond my understanding. I had walked in the church feeling one way, and I left there feeling so encouraged and strengthened. I was ready for what was to come.

The next morning, I woke up and got the kids ready for what I knew was going to be a very long day. We saw all of the family, friends, and members of the community. After all of this time we knew we were going to see Toia again. It was surreal to see her in a coffin. I never thought this would be a day I lived to see because I always thought that I would die before her. I saw my kids walk in and yes, they were sad, but at the same time they were strong and unmoved because they understood that Mommy was with the Lord in greater pastures. They became an anchor. I made the decision to remove them from the celebration service and take them to the office I had prepared with their games and the iPad because I did not want people projecting their grief on them. I wanted to protect them at that moment. I took advantage of this at moments because I needed a break from all the people that had come to the celebration service. It was a bit overwhelming. So, I just sat with them, waiting for the moment we were called out. The sanctuary was full. We had to place people in overflow rooms because so many people showed up.

The worship was so powerful that many people said to me they had never been at a funeral like this. I made sure to clarify that it was not come to a funeral, they came to a celebration. We celebrated my wife and that was all that I wanted: to worship Jesus and honor my wife. This was the best way to prepare for the new reality that was about to begin. It set the tempo for a lot of things in my life. The only thing I regret is not having thrown a party like this while she was alive so that she would have been able to see the amount of people that loved her. This, my dear reader, is something we should do for the ones we love.

"So, with you: now is your time of grief, but I will see you again and you will rejoice, and no one will take away your joy."

John 16:22

CHAPTER 4

THE UNSHARED PROCESS

Often times we've heard or read about the five or seven stages of grief which are: denial, anger, bargaining, depression, acceptance and hope, and processing grief.[1] But what I discovered is this timeline is for someone who is dying, not for the ones who are left behind when someone has died. Grief has no timeline. You don't wake up one day and say it's over. It continues for the rest of your life. It is the conversation that is ongoing. We always hear people say that "time heals all wounds." Well, that may not necessarily be the case. Grief just manifests itself in different ways. Time goes on. Grief is very different for someone in my position.

After everyone has gone home from the celebration, wake, or funeral, the cards, text messages, phone calls, visits (whether planned or unexpected). It just me, myself, and I. a man, as a man of faith, as a man who is leading people of faith in a pastoral leadership role, It

---

[1] https://www.hcf.com.au/health-agenda/body-mind/mental-health/moving-through-grief

looks very different. The challenge can be trying to step into a role that you're not meant to be in for the time. I had to learn how to step out of the pastoral role and just be a grieving husband. Often pastors go into auto-pilot. Being in pastoral ministry for as long as I've been, there is a default mode that kicks in the for the desire to serve by helping people even while you're bleeding. We make this mistake because of real life happening to us for suffering for the Gospel's sake. Many pastor serve while their marriages are on the rocks, losing a spouse or child, and continue to press forward in great error. Not allowing themselves to rest or receive counseling or therapy. We often forsake our humanity to attempt to be a superhero. There is a song from singer/songwriter KJ Scriven, called *Superman*. He reminds us that we are not strong enough to carry the load that only GOD can and that well I willingly have to take off the cap and try not be Superman.

It wasn't just that I lost my wife, I lost a way of life. I took a sabbatical from ministry for a year and a half. I needed to be with my children and just be dad. Everyday felt slower than usual. It seemed like the drag on forever. I had a conversation with my cousin Marissah and she revealed something that I never considered:

"You are now void of a time and space. Toia took up a time and space in your life that was filled for 21 years. Now that time and space is no longer filled up and it has created a vacuum in your life."

Any thing I did that seemed entertaining, I felt guilty for even being happy or wanting to share a laugh.

Everything feels empty. Everywhere I went, whether it was a new place or somewhere familiar, I always longed for her presence to be with me. Somehow, it would feel sweeter or more fulfilling if she was present. It was this dangerous place, because my family was at the center of everything and yet people could see my children playing and enjoying themselves and enjoy life to some extent, though we knew that there was a major shift in our lives.

"My flesh and my heart fail; But God is the strength of my heart and my portion forever."

Psalms 73:26 NKJV

CHAPTER 5

GRIEF AS A PUBLIC FIGURE AND A CHILD OF GOD

I didn't see myself as a public figure because I don't consider myself to be famous. I'm just a regular dude, or in this case, my wife and I were just regular people. Nevertheless, one of the things that I became fully aware of during my grief was that I am a public figure to some extent. For a long time, I lived very oblivious to it because I never gave it any attention or put much thought into it. I was never aware of the amount of people through the years had been observing us. I didn't realize that because of the spaces that I function, in some respects, we were in a lot of public platforms. Being a musician for 30+ years, a preacher, and on the pastoral team does put you in the public eye more often than not. Together with other public spaces we navigated, and the countless connections, we were favored to have a wide reach of influence with people. There were a lot of eyes upon us.

As a pastor there is an additional level of accountability as well as an expectation on how I should conduct myself in public and in private. It's even a biblical mandate and the scripture talks about how teachers are held more accountable than others (James 3:1). But I never put a whole lot of pressure on myself. Not that I didn't care about what people thought, I was mindful of how I was perceived, however, it did not rule my very being. I was just living life and trying to live in a way that was pleasing God.

But, having a role as a spiritual leader comes with many challenges. For example, often times we find ourselves in a position where we are preaching or teaching about something that we may not have gone through personally. It's in moments like mine with the loss of my wife where I've come to a place of wanting to live out the sermon that I've preached. This does not mean that I didn't do it before, but in my grieving process, everybody was watching. My responsibility was just to live, no words necessary, just live. Sometimes I felt pressure because I knew that every move I had to make needed to be a calculated move. Not that I was putting on a show or acting like I was some spiritual superhero, but just trying to live understanding that even in the midst of my greatest grief, somehow people were seeing me as an inspiration. To be honest with you, it's actually kind of confusing. How could I be seen as a leader, influencer, or an inspiration, while I'm just trying to navigate life as a grieving husband? Whether I understood it or not, that was my new reality. The preacher must now live the sermon. Achieving peace within the storm and trusting God in the process would testify to the faith I confessed.

Having what seems like all eyes on you—especially when tragedy strikes your household—can be overwhelming. Everybody is watching to see how you will respond. There were many people who were generally concerned about our well-being, which I am truly grateful for. However, I'm fully aware that there were many others who were watching just to see how I would respond concerning my life, but also, my faith in God. I think the thing that I was fully aware of has been understanding God's faithfulness even in tragedy. Often times we put our faith in God based on our tranquility. I've discovered that in these moments, this is where God proves who He is. When I made the announcement of my wife's passing on social media, the response that I received was quite beyond my understanding. There were so many tributes and kind words said about her and stories of things that she did for people that I didn't even know about. My timeline was filled with well wishes, prayers, condolences, and other acknowledgments concerning our family. To be honest, I was very overwhelmed by the response and humbled. To hear people talk about how they watched our lives and that we were an example to them was truly mind blowing. We never did or posted anything with the intention of becoming an example to others as a relationship goal. We simply loved each other, and many people noticed. The truth is that you never know who's watching you. This is why going through the grieving process publicly was a challenge. I knew that in the same manner people were observing our lives together, they would now be watching me and the moves and decisions I made. This included how I managed my grief and who I allowed to live the process with me.

It's been especially challenging considering that I am a widower. I can admit it is a very lonely place when the person I've created a rhythm of life with is suddenly is taken away from me. I have to do things alone now. You would be surprised at how many women who, on the outside seem concerned, but were really trying to prod to see if I was vulnerable or "thirsty" enough to take a drink from their well, all in hopes of becoming the *next Mrs. Williams*. This is not *plug and play*. 21 years of building a life is does not go away overnight nor would it be an easy transition. Its not just me, it's three children as well. Let's just say I'm a package deal.

It's kind of a wild scenario. I don't look at it from the angle as if I'm this ultra-desirable individual. I take into account that many had a front row seat to our marriage, and what they witnessed was happiness with each other. I loved her and I liked her, and there was nothing flaky about that. We weren't putting on a show. That was just how we rolled. In many ways, I'm grateful that people are able to see the genuineness of our relationship, and that many saw us as an example. So, knowing there are so many eyes on us, now on me, made me want to sometimes get away because I have felt so vulnerable since my wife died.

One of the biggest blessing is having accountability in my life. It doesn't have to be many, but enough to hold your feet to the fire, and make sure that you stay the course. I've been fortunate to have men who have lost their wives in my circle. Their insight and encouragement has helped me to see things from their vantage point. Much of our conversations where asking am I taking care of myself? To be honest, I didn't know what that looked like.

For at least the first year and a half, I didn't want to go out much locally. Concerts in the city, community events, and local gathers where I felt like was would see a lot people in whom I'm acquainted, I didn't feel like answering any questions about how I was feeling. I know people were genuinely concerned about us; however, I didn't have bandwidth to hold space with people.

As a leader, many people come to you for guidance in tough times, but now I had to figure out what to do as tragedy kicked down the door of my life. I thought about how I had to respond. Did I have the level of stoicism that seemed to be above reproach? There were many moments that I felt like falling apart but I felt that I didn't have that option. There are three kids that were and still are depending on me. Now I had to be the single father in the public eye. I not only have to be an example to them but also be an example at my church. I have to walk in this season in real-time. It is still hard to hear others say they admire my strength because there were so many times that I felt weak. I knew that everything I was achieving was all the Lord's doing. He has carried us through the whole thing; it has never been in my own strength but by the Lord's. I am fully aware we would not be where we are today had it not been through the guidance of his Spirit, covering our hearts and minds. I make sure to remember that God is faithful in all things; He will hide you, cover you and hover you under the shadow of His wings. It is an opportunity to tuck us away. Now, it's a matter of understanding the process that God has for my life and the life of my children and continuing to focus on that. Over time, things will be revealed.

CHAPTER 6

LOSING PILLARS & FIGHT, FLIGHT, OR FREEZE: WHICH DO YOU CHOOSE?

We hear the term, fight, flight, or freeze quite often. This term is used in regard to people and how they respond to adversity or tragedy. The people that fight are the ones that—regardless of what is surrounding them—stand firm and go against what may have been disrupted and try to bring order from chaos at all costs. Others flee from trouble and don't want to deal with it or hope that it disappears. Lastly, the people who freeze are gripped with anxiety to the point that they become paralyzed by everything that's going on around them and they are unable to fight. They are unable to even flee and get out of the way. They just become stuck there and become captive to the moment.

I can confess with all honesty I've been in all three at some stage of the process and still at some moments feeling like I'm dealing with all three at the same time. The *fight* in me always thinks about what my life should be and that I have to continue to live and move forward. The *flight* in me just wants to get away and take a break once in a while. The *freeze* in me becomes so overwhelmed that I feel like I can't do anything even though I can easily do the task. I just become overwhelmed with anxiety.

Trauma can render us feeling helpless and we will respond in these three ways. Fight, flight, or freeze.

I felt like losing my wife after seventeen years of marriage was the start of the chain of events that would alter my life moving forward. Then, six months later my father passed, and after another three months my grandmother passed away as well. Three major pillars in my life were gone within a nine-month period. It was bad enough that it felt like the ground was uneven already, but it felt like earthquakes were happening back-to-back. In many aspects, losing my wife brought this weight of expectation, to not only care for my children but now lead the household without the one who helped me build it. I felt like someone took her away from me. Losing my father to cancer brought me into a place where I now had to care for my mother while she was grieving the loss of both a daughter-in-law and her husband. Losing my grandmother, who was ninety-four, signified an end to a legacy that was left before us. Thankfully, I got to see her the day before she died. So, although it was an emotional day, I knew I had to be strong for my mother, who like me, lost all three together. My parents were the last people to see my wife and my mother had been by my father's side until the end. I had to be strong for her. All of this brought me closer and closer to being the only one standing. It felt like I had become the last line of defense, or as I would say, the last connection to my predecessors.

My father, Alonzo Williams, Sr. was not perfect by any stretch. My parents had a rocky married for early portion together and were separated for season because his poor decisions. But somewhere in GOD's plans, my parents reconnected and remained married another 26 years. One thing I know he did was work for a large portion of his life. There were only a few occasions where he was without a job. He was descent size 6 ft and the least 235 pounds and had what my uncles called "cornbread and syrup strength". Everyone who was close to him knew him as *Lonnie T* or *Lonnie*.

He had a ton of friends and people whom he's met over the years. He worked with youth for over 30 years of his life: coaching, mentoring, and counseling in various places of employment. His last job was working at an alternative school at risk student. That was his lane, working with people who needed guidance and he was gifted at it. I few years prior, he was just license as a minister of the Gospel. Life seemed like it was steadily trending in the right direction and then...he's gone. Just like that. My father whom I fostered a greater relationship in my later years...is gone.

So, what did I do? I fought hard to get a semblance of normalcy—or rather a new normal—because reality is nothing is going to be normal again. I felt very helpless. Of all of the people who were texting and calling right after the accident, only a few remained. It felt like someone pulled the carpet from under me. There was just a massive life change. I went from having support to supporting everybody else. It still feels like I have to hold up the places where these pillars were. I now have to be the pillar for my children with the absence of their mom. I have to be the pillar for my mom without my dad or grandmother present. All of this just got me thinking: what will be my go-to? What do I do with all of this? How do I respond when I feel helpless, and I feel like there are no answers or options? I felt like everything was falling apart and all of the weight was falling on me.

This was the season I knew I had to trust God even in the times it felt like He wasn't there. I knew there was no way that I would be able to walk while having to manage everything. I learned about my deficiencies and surrendered them to God. I saw His fidelity in all of my weaknesses. I went through a season of back-to-back bad news. I was afraid to say: what's next? First my wife passes, then my father gets sick and dies, my grandmother passes, and then the doctors discover that my daughter had an AVM in her brain (Arteriovenous malformation—look that up on your spare time) after the accident. It was just devastating and over time, I felt I didn't have the strength to continue fighting. I went from fight to freeze in some extent. I felt like every time I made a move, something happened. I was a shell of my former self. You could say that I was on autopilot. Just going through the motions. It was hard to grasp this season and not everyone around me understood all of what I was carrying. There is nothing more confusing than people who would come to me thinking they are "encouraging" me with phrases like, "Your strength is encouraging me," "I love that you are such a strong example," or "God recruits His strongest soldiers for the hardest battles." I could go on, but you get the point. Externally, I may have looked okay, but internally, I was literally hollow and falling to pieces.

CHAPTER 7

THE SUBTLE REMINDERS: EMOTIONAL LANDMINES

In some countries where years of war have taken place, there are a number of dangerous undetonated devices still lying dormant. And every so often, you hear a story about a hiker, or an outdoors person accidentally stepping on a landmine and tragically lose their life. A landmine is an explosive charge concealed just under the surface of the ground or of a roadway, designed to be detonated by pressure, proximity of a vehicle or person, etc. The whole purpose of it being concealed is that the enemy doesn't know where they are located.

> **Emotional Landmine**: *A random outburst of emotion drawn from a moment or memory.*

Emotional landmines become a part of your everyday life after you lose a loved one. They come in various forms: it could be a place, a smell, a texture, a food item, a picture, an article of clothing. You don't even know you stepped on it until it explodes. You can look at a picture a thousand times without a response. And then one day, you look at the picture and burst into tears. Or you could go to a familiar place that reminds you of a past memory, and your mood changes immediately. All of these are examples of emotional landmines.

When I stepped into the house for the first time after the accident, it felt like a vacuum sucked all the life out the house. On the refrigerator, we have a family calendar. I will keep my own personal calendar on the phone, but I would put anything that I had on the family calendar for everyone to see.

It was Toia's idea, because our lives became very busy between work, ministry, kid's events, appointments, significant people's birthdays, to-do list, and the list goes on. We lived by that calendar. It kept structure for our household. When we returned home, we continued using the calendar to keep track of life. If it isn't broken, there's no need to change what has been established. However, as time went on, as each month went by, I would see less and less of her handwriting in which she had written in future events and appointments. It became more and more apparent that she was gone. Every time I changed the month, my heart became more and more burdened with grief. I actually kept the calendar from 2021, knowing it was the last time that I would see her handwriting. Putting up a new calendar and starting a new year was heartbreaking knowing that nothing on the calendar would have her handwriting on it, just mine. To be honest with you, it doesn't feel like the new year starts on January 1. For me, the calendar starts on June 19. Grief has the ability to shift the new year.

In the grieving process, the administrative changes are probably the most unspoken and stressful part of the grieving. From changing the names on bills, bank accounts, investments, car notes, leases, shutting down any subscriptions, or even completing with their place of employed, become emotionally taxing because you're constantly having to explain the reason why you changing or removing a name. It's being traumatized over and over again and reminding yourself that the person that you're doing these things for is now gone. Honestly, I don't know how I did it. This is a part of the *fight mode* in me that wants to get it done and get it out the way so that I could rest. But I discovered that's an illusion. There is always something that comes up. It will remind you that your loved one is gone.

One of the most traumatizing moments I experienced was when I went to pick up my daughter from her robotics club practice. I left bible study to pick up and bring her back with me to finish bible study and dropped her off to Youth Ministry. As I was driving downtown to York City from North George Street, I would have to pass the cemetery where my wife was laid to rest. As I was turning, a vehicle turned in front of me. The vehicle was a white compact car. When I looked closer, it was a Kia Septra—the same car that my family and I were in during the crash! So...I'm riding down the street behind this car that is the exact make and model of the vehicle my wife died while riding down the street next to the cemetery were my wife's remains rest. I couldn't do anything but let the tears flow. I stopped the car to allow this wave to wash over me.

CHAPTER 8

LOSING THE MOTHER
I ONCE KNEW

Loses are never easy, and as you have been reading so far, I have gone through so many. You would think that I would be able to manage the subject with better ease. The truth is every loss is different, and we deal with them in a variety of ways. Losing a parent was difficult enough, but watching someone you love begin to lose their sense of self is even more difficult. I feel so helpless watching and waiting day by day as my mother's mental health was becoming more and more unstable.

If I can speak from the heart, I really don't know what to make of the last two years. I had so many people removed from my life in a short amount of time. My mom has remained just off center of me because she was losing people as well. She lost her daughter-in-law, her husband, and her mother. She had to be strong, and even though I truly won't ever know how hard it has been, I have watched her recently begin to lose her memory and struggle with mental health. She has gone from being this vibrant woman who was full of life, always very active in community activities, baking and cooking while serving and caring for people, to slowly dimming to a point that I feel I may lose her soon. At the very least, I am losing the mom I used to know.

All of this started to show prior to the accident, but since my dad was her primary caregiver, it did not seem so evident. Now, due to all of the losses that occurred, things accelerated very quickly. I started to see the signs after my aunt Barb began so see how my mom behavior had changed. She was the caregiver to my grandparent who suffered with and died from Dementia and Alzhteimer's.

She was a very sharp person who most of her life had clerical positions, including working at a bank which required that sharpness and talent. She was the first African-American teller at the bank in her home town of Oxford, PA, and she had to face a lot of pressure. On another occasion, she took a position in the School District of Lancaster (PA) where I grew up and remained with the school district for over twenty-five years with a well-known reputation of being a great employee who was held with high regard. My mom was married for forty-seven years. She was a Sunday School teacher, worship leader, she did Girl Scouts and sports. She sewed, made clothes, tailored suits and dresses for some side money.

I've had to witness her mental capacity decline at a very rapid pace. It has been very challenging for me and frustrating to live in a city thirty min-utes away and have to care for my own household at the same time. I am thankful for God and a special group of friends that made themselves present to help me with the medical care. With the correct diagnosis and care, my mom has been pulling through beautifully. Knowing that my mom is being taken care of takes a huge weight of my shoulders, not because I don't enjoy doing it myself, but because there are more people by her side to do so. Her care facility is just seven minutes away from my church, so this has also been a blessing because I am able to see her every week. Because of the nearness, she has also gained a new church family who have embraced her like they did my family.

> I have been young, and now am old; yet have I not seen the righteous forsaken, nor his seed begging bread.

I am thankful that my mom is still here physically. Even though she does not have all of her mental facul-ties, she still has a mind that worships God, which is amazing. Although she has aged and has gone through the traumas, she still has a pretty active life. She walks on a regular basis and loves to be physically active at her capacity.

This tells us that even though we are not able to care for ourselves, God's promises make themself present. He is able to still care for us, even when we can't take care of ourselves.

With it all, I know that there are different blessings that come with every season. I am always reminded that God will give us the strength to persist and resist all types of loses. It still hurts, it's still a challenge, but as the word of God says in Psalms 37:25, "I have been young, and now am old; yet have I not seen the righteous forsaken, nor his seed begging bread."

CHAPTER 9

LOSS FROM THE EYES OF A CHILD

For this part of the book, I decided to include this bonus section because our loss as a family also included the pain and trauma of our children. My oldest, Beautiful, my oldest son and middle child, Trenton, and my youngest son, Marquis, who are now 15, 13, and 11 years old at the time of this publishing. I wanted to share thoughts and experiences, because everything looks different from the eyes of a child. My children were a big reason for fighting so hard to get my body back back as close to *normal* as I could. They were were moving forward playing with friends, going back to doing to their normal routine without missing beat. This was the tempo my children set for me and my job was to keep up with with pace.

My oldest daughter had trauma in the way of not remembering the event. She is only able to remember three hours before the crash and then waking up hours after the surgery. She sat behind my wife in the car when we were hit. She took a blunt force trauma, which cause memory to lapse in the of a day and 1/2. She is a daddy's girl. I know this for sure. As I've observed her these past few years, she has displayed a level of resilience that I can only thank GOD for. She has a weird sense of humor, like her father, in which she shares certain jokes with me that if she told other people, they would be horrified. I just say to myself, "A can't deny that's my child (LOL)." She is like her mother in many ways: very intelligent, active in a bunch of activities, and has interest in a lot of creative ways. She has her mother's intelligence and her daddy's wit—a very dangerous combination.

Trenton, the middle child, is the child who is very "black and white" when it comes to life. He showed a level of leadership and resolved through this ordeal that has blown my mind to say the least. In my conversations with him over the last year or so, he's been very stoic and hasn't missed a beat. He is artistic and creative, but is structured (as much as a 13-year-old can be). They He is like me in a different way—asking a lot of questions. He never questions his mother's death or why. Not because wasn't allowed to, but a simple declaration he made while I was in hospital: "I'm sad, but mommy is with the LORD now." This stood out for a number of reasons. If my children, who are losing a primal relationship are able to bounce back and keep rolling forward, how much more do I need to stay the course?

These are the words of my youngest son, Marquis. He has been the most expressive about losing his mother. He is the baby of the house was a momma's boy. This was hard for him. Over time, I began to see the effect of losing his mother took on him. I've really have had my greatest adjustments as a parent with him, keeping stern in some moments while being bit more nurturing in other. These are things you learn as you go along. Here ye him:

"I was eight years old when the accident happened. I remember we went to some events with my mom and dad and my siblings that day. I don't remember much from the accident, but I still remember the physical impact of the other car on ours. I tried to move and get out of the car, but I physically couldn't until a person came and helped me out. I felt very weak and confused because I didn't know what had just happened. I was taken from the scene of the accident on a helicopter because my injuries were very bad.

When I was able to walk out of the hospital, I learned that all five of us where in the accident, but only four of us made it out alive. Having to go visit dad at the hospital and hear that mom died was very hard. I had lost my mommy. We stayed at grandpop and grandmom's house, and we didn't really do much for a while but sit on the sofa. I felt terrible.

Now, after some time has passed, I really miss the things I did with mommy like play tennis, game, and movie nights. Also, it's sad for me to think of the things we don't get to do with her because she is gone. If I could talk to mommy, I would tell her that I love her and that I wish she was here."

CHAPTER 10

BECOMING TREVOR 3.0 (THE MOSAIC)

*Therefore, if anyone is in Christ, he is a
new creation; old things have passed away;
behold, all things have become new.*

(2 Corinthians 5:17)

In my season of loss, this is probably the hardest part I have had to embrace. When I think about operating systems or phones, there is always a new update that needs to be upgraded. When you decide to install the update, you have to put the phone down, plug it in, and let it sit for the time the update and changes require. It tells you what the upgrades will be and in what area.

The thing about God is that when He wants to bring the 'new' in your life, you don't know how those upgrades are going to come. Often, you might not even be told what those things or changes are going to do. I had to recognize in this season of my life, with all of the

61

loses and now dealing with my mother's mental health issues as well as my daughter's brain surgery after the accident, it was a lot of weight to carry. It was pressing on me in a way I couldn't even fathom. I don't know how I made it here. I know it was with God's help, but I can't describe the step by step process the got me to this point. It was crazy how all of these things have changed the way I think about things, the perspective of how I see the world and my relationship with God. It's all different. Things on the other side are different. In many areas, it's just the little things. I went from being a husband to a widower; from having a partner to share their life with, to being a single father. Now, I also transitioned from a son to a full caretaker for my mother with all of the responsibility that is required. Having been such an independent person, I now have learned to delegate and ask for help. Even in ministry my approach is a bit different. I feel more precise in my availability, in the sense of managing all of the roles with a good balance to be present in ministry but be present with my family.

I recognize that there were a lot of things that I need to change and balance. My time is one of them. I have learned that my time is valuable. Losing loved ones automatically starts a morality clock in all of us. I do not know how much time I have left. The reality is that when you face death so closely, you realize that you can't afford to waste time. So, there are times when I feel sense of urgency, but at the same time, I have to make sure I don't let anxiety consume me. My therapist said to me: *"you have to learn to live in the moment."* It really hit home because I knew that there were a lot of things in my life where I was starting to get anxious. I was wanting to be in three different places at the same time. I had to learn how to slow down and be where my feet are. It was a profound revelation for me. I needed to be present in the place where my feet were.

The second thing that has been profound in my life is I *can't make future decisions based off of other's grief*

This took a lot of time to come to this place but I've had to understand that everyone is going to have all of these different exceptions for my life and the only person(s) who should have major input in your life is YOU!! We can make the mistake being more mindful of others grief, that it did not allow me to fully feel because I was the "strong one" for everybody. But who is gonna be strong for me?

Now, let's step back and understand. There is safely of designated people in your life who you are able to take things through the filter. Your accountability will help you navigate, pray, guide, and discern what things are healthy and what is potentially destructive. But good friends will allow you the space to allow GOD to work on your heart and mind, but present enough that they are not crowding you.

This has been a blessing for me in this season of my life. There is so much currently going on and at the same time, there is so much that God has shown me. I have areas that need to be patched up in my spiritual and emotional walk and capacity. Before I am able to reach a place where I can open the door to a new relationship,

I need to make sure I come from a place of healing and knowing what is real or not. Speaking truthfully, the world is full of good people, but not all those good people are good for you. Today, I have a lot on my plate, and I am a package deal. I don't come alone. That in itself is another reality.

The new me is very different and I need to be more direct in some regards. If I find out the intentions are ill, I have no issues saying goodbye. Some other aspects are realizing that I downplay what God has given me and I have to learn to walk comfortably in that. I had a wife who supported and cared for me and the condition of my soul for twenty years of my life. It's tough now not having a person to bounce of those ideas. The little things like not having the immediate response to having someone ask *how was your day?* Or simple things like, *what's for dinner?* Now I have to step into those things alone. It has been an interesting transition into a new me in many ways. Sometimes, it has been scary because we never know what we are capable of until we are forced to do things. It's having the fear of failing but also the fear of succeeding because expectations come with that. Even for this book you hold in your hands today, I am excited for it, but I also have anxiety about it as well.

I am learning to live in the moment. The new me does look different. I have to take people through the filters and set boundaries and levels of accountability. I no longer have the coverage of my wife, so I am responsible to take care of my heart and my soul. I'm not going to allow anyone to come in and break down what has been established already. The new me has to become a new dad in a way that I am able to step into my children's life in a new way and have different conversations with them that I normally would not have. I have to manage the tensions of being nurturing as well as being the disciplinarian, which I was accustom. Now, have to create a new level of accountability from my closest friends, but also from people that have my best interest in ministry whether it be my pastor or my business partners.

My children are also good at keeping me humble and give me their honest opinions. They don't care if I am a minister of the Gospel, a pastor, a musician, a public speaker, and now, an author. They will make sure I take care of their needs: have dinner on the table, take them to school on time, and know where we are going to vacation, or what we will do throughout the week. In all of those small things, they make sure I keep up.

Real life. I have fostered an even better relationship with them in this new season. As a father I have to be their starting point and model a Christ-like lifestyle. I want them to be their best selves and cultivate a loving household.

I have had to discover new things about myself. What I like and what I don't like. I have discovered some things that I did not do well while I was with my wife. I have also made it an intention to do things that maybe in the past I didn't do out of respect for my wife or because we disagreed on them. I have found new liberty but within the parameters of a Godly man. I do have new ventures and new ideas that I am able to step into and I think that this area of my life is still a work in progress. I am discovering new things every day. I still have the same goals, but it shifts because now I have to operate in a different way. God has had to download new things in me through His word and wisdom, and through conversations with different people who are vested in my life. I have had to do a change in mindset. It will continue to unfold because this is the chapter of my life that I am currently building: Trevor 3.0. There will be changes and upgrades to come with each new day as things are added to my life in real time. This chapter does not end, it is more of a *to be continued*.

I know that I will still make mistakes, and learn new things, but I trust that God will guide me through this new season.

The one thing that I can say is that being in the gray area, it helps to develop depth and texture to continue the conversation that defined the title of this book.

Josh Heckert, who is a prolific expressional painter and my tattoo artist, said to me that in painting, when you mix the black and white it creates texture and depth. This season of my life is creating both. Texture in the way of how people can tangibly feel what's going on with me, the words that I say and the actions that I take. I pray that people can actually feel and touch my takeaways from the book and that they can put into actions in their own process. And depth, meaning that I have the capacity or have a place where I can pour deep well of God's wisdom and understanding, even discernment, about life and how it presents itself. There is a deep depository of the things that are within us. Although this book may come to an end, our books continue to be written.

I pray that you all meet the God of the gray area.

This chapter does not end, it is more of a *to be continued.*

ACKNOWLEDGEMENTS

To my late father, Alonzo Williams Sr.:

I've seen your life in quite a few phases, many of them challenging and often met with much adversity. Sometimes, those trials were self-inflicted. Nevertheless, I saw when you allowed the Lord to do some transformative work in your life. I saw it allows you to help to transform others lives as well, and it showed me that regardless of what you do that God can still use you even when you've messed up very badly. I have other siblings because of choices that you made, I don't hold that against you. It makes things complex at times, but in God's grace, I was able to learn from the lessons of your mistakes and triumphs. The last six months that you were alive were the most critical part of my life. I saw you be there for me and your grandchildren. You kept things in order and put people in their place when it could've been chaos that was floating around us after Toia's death. Thank you for enduring and running the race that was set before you.

To my Late grandmother, Mary "Betty" Harris:

You were the last of my grandparents to leave this earth, I can say that I've had the privilege of having both sets of my grandparents in my life. The last season, I really didn't grasp the totality of that until now. Losing you in a time when I was enduring so much and I really didn't have the chance to really take a deep breath and take the notion that you were gone. You always had something to say and most times it was really, really funny. You would say things that we wouldn't expect you to say, and it would catch everybody off-guard. You filled up the room with laughter and also comical arguing with Pop Pop, who proceeded you. I would tell people watching you guys was like watching a great black sitcom at the levels of the Cosby show. Every time I was around you guys it was always something different and something memorable. I hope I've made you proud.

To Redemption International Ministries:

Thank you, Pastor Danny Haas, and the Redemption family for the opportunity and the privilege of being in pastoral ministry to great people who in my worst times stood up and girded us with prayer, wrapped your arms around us, and served our family as we endure major losses and major trials in such a short amount of time. LaToia, and I along with our children, grew spiritually as a family, served, laughed, cried, prayed, and fellowship with you. I will not forget the 12 years we shared.

The Chapel Harrisburg:

Thank you, Pastor Larry and Lady Julia family for a new start of my life and being a godly steward of my soul in the season of transition. You have helped me to be more refined in my spiritual life, being detailed about protecting the delicate parts of my spiritual life. This part of my life I've had to discover who I am, and who God is made me to be. Thank you for challenging me and causing me to grow in very detailed and unchecked spaces in my life. It's been a healthy journey so far and I'm excited to see what the Lord does with the journey ahead.

Juanita Glover:

I can only imagine having to lay a child to rest when it seemed as though she was in the prime of her life. There are so many questions that don't have answers. Yet you have persevered with very challenging days. You could have easily emotionally checked out. But you continue to be a great help to me and your grandchildren while you were caring the heavy burden of your grief. Thank you for the meals, stepping in doing laundry when I didn't have time, taking the kids when I had to go out of town for work, or ministry related endeavors. You've been one of my greatest supports as we've had to lean on each other at times through the hardest days of our life. I love you very much.

Antoine RJ Wright:

We have been friends for almost 25 years. You are my brother and my best friend. You have seen me and my best and worst. I am beyond wealthy, having a friend who has been there every step of the way. You were the only single friend who I would take marriage advice from simply because you knew both Toia and I from the time we met (in fact, we all met the same day). You are the godfather of my children and I would not trust them in the hands of anyone else. You are always uncle Antoine to them because more importantly you've been my brother for all these years.

To all who are part of the network of friends, family member, colleagues (professionally or meeting in my travels) There are too many of you to name. Otherwise, I would have to write a whole other book if I wanted to detail all the people who played significant parts in this continued healing journey of my life. What I can say is all of you have made some contribution to this book. Though may or may not be written somewhere in these chapters, know that they are etched in the annals of my heart and mind. I am always reminded to remain grateful for those who cooked a meal for my family, sewed financially, continually praying for us, sending encouraging words, sharing your testimony about how our lives have impacted you.

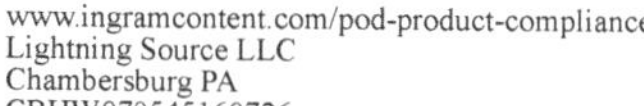

* 9 7 9 8 2 1 8 4 6 1 7 1 3 *